ACTIVATING GOD'S DIVINE PROTECTION

ACTIVATING GOD'S DIVINE PROTECTION

Psalm 91 Revealed

HERMAN (DUSTY) SHELTON

XULON PRESS

Xulon Press
2301 Lucien Way #415
Maitland, FL 32751
407.339.4217
www.xulonpress.com

Paperback ISBN-13: 978-1-66282-562-0
Ebook ISBN-13: 978-1-66282-563-7

CONTENTS

Preface

HAVE YOU EVER wondered if there is any place in the world that is safe from all the mounting dangers in this increasingly chaotic world? The coronavirus (COVID-19) is the latest thing to bring fear to the world, and we wouldn't want to be caught in one of those riots they show on the news either. Situations and circumstances seem to be changing on a dime. So, where can one find safety and protection?

There is a safe place that you and your household can go to and reside at any time. God tells you where that place is in Psalm 91. In fact, you don't have to actually go anywhere to be in that safe place. It can be wherever you are right now, even if it doesn't *seem* to be safe at the moment. God wants you to be safe 24/7, and He tells us in Psalm 91 just how to acquire that protection.

My writing is a compilation of spiritual truths regarding what Psalm 91 states about victory over sickness, accidents, and catastrophes. Even though the plague and the pestilence are mentioned as something from which God will protect us, there is so much more to His protection.

I started studying and teaching Psalm 91 at the local detention center, where I have been a minister for over twenty years. In March 2020, COVID-19 arrived in our area, and its presence prevented our ministry team from continuing to teach at the facility. However, I felt compelled to keep studying Psalm 91 on my own. I didn't expect my studies to turn into a book at the time, but the more I studied, the more notes I took. The more notes I took, the more I studied. I realized God was trying to make a point. He wants us to know that He wants to protect us, and He will if we follow His instructions.

This book is not copied from anyone else's work; it is completely original. It is meant to be an interdenominational message, one that can be applied to the life of any Christian. In addition, I have included instructions on how one who is not a Christian can enter into and receive this protection as well.

I used Scripture to support everything I've written. My hope is that you, the reader, will receive it in the spirit it was written—simply to help you learn how to survive anything the devil throws at you and how to receive everything God promises according to Scripture. I chose to use the King James Version (KJV) throughout because I have found people prefer and trust it the most. I realize many of the words used in the KJV may not be easily understandable, or they may have different meanings today. Don't worry. I have looked up specific words and have noted the proper definitions for easy comprehension.

I could have made this book three times as long, but I didn't want to weary the reader. Some books, I feel, just have more information than is necessary, so my goal was to stop when the point was clearly delivered. In addition, I wanted it to be short enough to reread often. I have reread a number of books several times because they just give my faith a boost. I also aspired to make it a true pocket book. That way one can easily carry it in a pocket or purse as a handy reference guide and faith builder to recharge one's faith like a weak battery can be recharged.

As I studied and meditated on this psalm, I became more and more excited because I began to realize that God revealed how we can receive His divine protection in just sixteen verses. As you read along, you will discover, as I have, that there is a breadth, length, depth, and height to this song. Psalm 91 is like striking a gold mine with sixteen veins (verses) of gold, and each vein has more veins branching off of it. The fruit of this psalm is better than fine gold, and it gets richer and purer with each strike of the pick.

God's protection has been here all this time, but unless we unearth the treasure, it stays buried, or, as one could say—it's just words on a page. It is inactive in our lives until we understand how to apply it. My goal is to highlight and dig out the treasure of truth that I found hidden in Psalm 91 so that you can apply it to your life and live out God's promises. When you do what Psalm 91 suggests, you can be confident that you will have the full protection it promises.

INTRODUCTION

PSALM 91 IS not a prayer. It is a proclamation, something we say (decree or declare), and it is something we believe by faith. Our faith-filled words activate God's power. We use our faith and our voice to activate the Word of God. We cannot just mentally agree with it. We must speak it. If we want the protection offered in this psalm, we have to SAY, DO, and BELIEVE something to activate it. The blessings in Psalm 91 are completely contingent upon the believer acting upon the promises. So, as they say, it's all up to you.

No less than seven times, God spoke something into existence. The eighth time God spoke something into existence, He said: *Let us make man in our own image and after our likeness; and let them have dominion* (Gen. 1:26). God spoke everything into existence, and then He created us in His own image. What if God had just thought these things and not spoken them? God spoke, and when He did, it became so. Do you see the similarities of us being made in His image?

Because God created us in His image as speaking spirits, our words have power! Therefore, we are created to speak certain words, especially His words. Psalm 91 informs us to speak the truth (decree) and believe it (by faith). When we do, the living Word will become activated as a fulfilled promise in our lives, and it will keep us safe from any and all physical or spiritual attacks of the enemy. This encompasses any sickness, disease, or calamity, day or night. Yes, this psalm states all that, and that's how it's done.

It is important to understand that you can't get the full impact or the entirety of the promise by just singling out and confessing a particular line or verse. If you want God's full protection, it must be done His way.

Each verse has other verses thrown in for support, and each verse builds on the preceding one, making it stronger like the building of a house. Just one wall standing alone is easy to knock over, but as the house is built, as each piece of timber and wall are connected, it becomes stronger and stronger. I want your faith to be so strong that you will never doubt, even when the devil comes at you like a roaring lion. When you speak God's words in faith, the devil runs off in fear. *Submit yourselves therefore to God. Resist the devil, and he will flee from you* (James 4:7).

I see Psalm 91 as a type of preventive maintenance. It prevents every evil thing from coming upon us. As we go through the verses, you will see that they cover anything and everything that could harm a child of God anywhere and at any time, day or night. For instance, if you are prevented from getting the plague (*see* Ps. 91:10), you don't need someone to lay hands on you and pray the prayer of faith for you to be healed. *They shall lay hands on the sick, and they shall recover* (Mark 16:19). You missed getting sick because you acted on the blessings of the promises; therefore, you didn't need prayer for healing.

While I was in the Navy, I was in the aircraft fire department, and we had to do regular preventive maintenance on the fire trucks we were assigned to. This meant we had to do daily checks on them to make sure everything was in working order in case of an emergency. It wouldn't be good if the battery was low so a truck wouldn't start or if a truck ran out of gas on the way to an emergency. They absolutely had to work when needed. This is what I mean by doing preventive maintenance. We can do preventive maintenance that can, figuratively speaking, prevent us from having a dead battery or running out of gas in an emergency. Psalm 91's truth actually prevents bad things from happening to us at any time, even in an emergency.

As you read this book and meditate on God's Word, my prayer is that you will receive divine revelation and the faith of Christ to believe God for every one of His truths and promises found in Psalm 91.

PSALM 91

[1] *He that dwelleth in the secret place of the Most High shall abide under the shadow of the Almighty.*

[2] *I will say of the Lord, He is my refuge and my fortress: my God; in him will I trust.*

[3] *Surely He shall deliver thee from the snare of the fowler, and from the noisome pestilence.*

[4] *He shall cover thee with His feathers, and under His wings shalt thou trust: His truth shall be thy shield and buckler.*

[5] Thou shalt not be afraid for the terror by night; nor for the arrow that flieth by day;

[6] Nor for the pestilence that walketh in darkness; nor for the destruction that wasteth at noonday.

[7] A thousand shall fall at thy side, and ten thousand at thy right hand; but it shall not come nigh thee.

[8] Only with thine eyes shalt thou behold and see the reward of the wicked.

[9] Because thou hast made the Lord, which is my refuge, even the Most High, thy habitation;

[10] There shall no evil befall thee, neither shall any plague come nigh thy dwelling.

[11] For He shall give His angels charge over thee, to keep thee in all thy ways.

[12] They shall bear thee up in their hands, lest thou dash thy foot against a stone.

[13] Thou shalt tread upon the lion and adder: the young lion and the dragon shalt thou trample under feet.

[14] Because He hath set his love upon Me, therefore will I deliver him: I will set him on high, because he hath known My name.

[15] He shall call upon Me, and I will answer him: I will be with him in trouble; I will deliver him, and honour him.

[16] With long life will I satisfy him, and shew him My salvation.

1

Qualified to Receive

THERE ARE TWENTY-THREE promises in a total of sixteen verses in Psalm 91, and there are certain conditions that must be met in order to apply the truth. Doing what Psalm 91 says is the only way to receive God's protection anywhere, at any time, and from anything. I will list the promises all throughout, and you can check the conditions as you read them.

God is your ever-present, Most High, and Almighty protector. There is none higher or mightier. If He can't do it, it can't be done. God is the ultimate superhero. Lois Lane had Superman, but we have a super God! Our God is not moved or changed by anything or anyone. God, unlike Superman, has no weaknesses, so kryptonite doesn't affect Him either.

As I wrote in the introduction, Jesus said we can lay hands on the sick, and they will recover. However, what is better than recovering from sickness is not getting sick to begin with. This amazing psalm, designed by God, can actually prevent sickness and other calamities before they can come upon us. As you will see, it is all up to you to do what God instructs. The rest is up to Him.

You might ask, "If that is so, why hasn't Psalm 91 protected me or others all along?" There are reasons why, and it's not because God is picking and choosing. Neither is it that God loves one more than another. God does not show favoritism as He is no respecter of persons (*see* Acts 10:34).

In order to apply Psalm 91 to your life, you must fear (have a reverential fear of) God, make Jesus your Lord and Savior, and then decree and believe it. When this psalm is spoken and believed by faith, it is activated for you, the believer. Jesus said anything will be possible to those with faith as a grain of mustard seed (*see* Mark 11).

Scripture states to fear only God, never man (or anything else in the natural). *And the Lord commanded us to do all these statutes, to fear the Lord our God, for our good always, that He might preserve us alive, as it is at this day* (Deut. 6:24).

In fact, there are at least forty-five scriptures in the Bible that instruct us to fear God, and there are none that instruct us to fear anything or anyone else. Jesus made no bones about it: *But I say unto you My friends, be not afraid of them that kill the body, and after that they have no more that they can do. But I will forewarn you whom you should fear: Fear Him, which after He has killed has power to cast into hell; yea, I say unto you, fear Him* (Luke 12:4–5).

God accepts and protects those who fear Him. *But in every nation that fears Him, and works righteousness, is accepted of Him* (Acts 10:35).

Scripture tells us that the Lord hears the prayers of the righteous. *For the eyes of the Lord are over the righteous, and His ears are open unto their prayers...*(1 Peter 3:12; *see* John 9:31 and 1 John 5:15).

How can one be righteous to have his or her prayers heard and answered when Isaiah 64:6 asserts that we are all unclean and our righteousness is like filthy rags? We get and have our righteousness only from and in Jesus. *For He has made Him to be sin for us, who knew no sin; that we might be made the righteousness of God in Him* (2 Cor. 5:21). Under the Mosaic covenant (the law), not one could be righteous. Under the new covenant, we may all become righteous when we accept Jesus as our Lord and Savior.

Jehovah God has many names. Maybe you have heard of some of them. I suggest you get to know ALL the names of God because His names are who He is and what He does. Here are a few of my favorite names of God that relate especially to Psalm 91:

1. Jehovah Ropheka—I am the Lord who heals thee (*see* Ex. 15:26).

2. Jehovah Jireh—I am the God who provides (*see* Ex. 22:14).

3. Jehovah Rohi—I am the Good Shepherd (*see* Ps. 23 and 91).

You may know Him as God, but you need to get to know Him particularly as Jehovah Rohi. The Good Shepherd (Jesus) is charged with protecting His sheep. Jesus calls His beloved His sheep. The Good Shepherd is faithful to fully protect His sheep. Again, that's who He is, and that's what He does. Psalm 91 is about 24/7 protection for you or anyone else who activates it.

You can meet Jehovah Rohi in Psalm 91. You can become one of His sheep and receive His protection. He tells you just how. Romans 10:9 explains exactly how Jesus can be your Lord and Savior: *That if thou shall confess with thy mouth the Lord Jesus, and believe in thy heart, that God has raised a Him from the dead, thou shall be saved.* When we receive Jesus as our Lord and Savior, we become a son or daughter of God—a believer. Jesus becomes Jehovah Rohi, the Good Shepherd, to us. I will cover this matter in more detail as we go along.

You must believe (have faith), and you must trust God. Without faith, it is impossible to please God (*see* Heb. 11:6). An example of God's stance on having faith is the account of the Roman centurion. The centurion's servant was healed by Jesus when the guard believed

5

(had faith) that Jesus could and would heal him. In fact, Jesus marveled at the centurion, and He said, *I tell you, not even in Israel have I found such faith* (*see* Luke 7:1–10).

You can begin to see why many people aren't protected. They do not fear God, they haven't received their righteousness by making Jesus their Lord and Savior, and they lack faith. We will learn how to activate the promises by acting on the blessings in order to receive the promises. This is just how God works.

2

Our Responsibility

PSALM 91 IS comprised of two segments: our part and God's part. We are only responsible for our part, and we can and are to fully trust God to fulfill His portion—for the Word of God is upright and never fails (*see* Ps. 33:4; Luke 1:37). God is trustworthy. *God is not a man, that he should lie; neither the son of man, that he should repent: hath he said, and shall he not do it? Or hath he spoken and shall he not make it good?* (Num. 23:19) This scripture tells us that unlike anyone else, God is completely trustworthy.

Let's dig out some of the treasures found in Psalm 91, beginning with our responsibility. Our part in this protection covenant is expressed in verses 1 and 2. As you read along, note carefully *he who dwells* and *he who says*. This is our responsibility under the terms of the covenant in order to release God's power to fulfill His promises.

> **Psalm 91:1—***He that dwells in the secret place of the Most High shall abide under the shadow of the Almighty.*

He (this is you, male or female)—This applies to anyone who will do what this psalm requires. This means it is your responsibility to do what it says. As I said earlier, there are things you must say and do in order for it to work for you. No one can do it for you.

That dwells—To dwell is to live in or at a specified place. God could be saying, "It's nice of you to drop in occasionally, but I'd rather you come and live here."

In the secret place—This is a personal, private place with God, a shelter really. Only God sees you in the secret place. This secret place can be a literal time and place. It is wise and helpful to have a factual place to go to in order to be alone with God. Jesus often went to a mountain or a *certain place* where He could be alone with the Father to pray. *But thou, when thou prayest, enter into thy closet, and when thou hast shut the door, pray to thy Father which is in secret; and thy father which sees in secret shall reward thee openly* (Matt. 6:6). This is an example to us.

If possible, you should set up a special time to be with God in your secret place. A specified time will help keep you accountable. So, get alone and quiet with God. Any quiet area in your house such as a closet, den, porch, or any other area where you can be alone with God will do. The importance of the secret place is not about the actual place itself—what it looks like or where it is. This is also a spiritual place to meet with God. Jesus spoke of a certain place to worship Him, but He also said we should worship Him in spirit and in truth (*see* John 4:20–24).

In emergency cases, it can be anywhere at any time. It will still work in these times. It is always good to know well or have memorized this psalm so that you can have it work for you when you don't have a written copy available.

We go to the secret place not only to speak to God but also to hear from Him. We can hear from God. Even though He is a big God, He speaks in a still, small voice (*see* 1 Kings 19:12). When I was teaching at the detention center, I taught that there are three ways to hear God's voice:

1. Get close. His whisper cannot be heard unless we are close to Him. We get close to God by reading the Word of God, praying, praising Him, and teaching or preaching. Doing spiritual things can also bring us closer to God.

2. Get quiet. We cannot hear His still, small voice with the television blaring. If we are surfing the web, it may be quiet on the outside; however, we are not being quiet on the inside. We cannot hear Him if we aren't quiet.

3. Listen. After we have gotten close and quiet, we listen. I have been in the same room while my wife was calling out my name, but I didn't

hear her. I wasn't listening; I was either watching television or talking to someone else.

Of the Most High (not the Almost High, but the Most High)—There is none higher in authority or power than God. In Hebrew, the name of God here is El-Elyon, and it always refers to the highest sovereignty of the heavens and earth. In Genesis 14:18–22 alone, Most High is used four times when referring to God:

> *Melchizedek was priest of the most high God...Blessed be Abram of the most high God, possessor of heaven and earth. He is the most high God, who has delivered his enemies into His hand...Abram lifted up his hand and swore unto the Lord, the most high God, the possessor of heaven and earth.*

Shall abide—The definition of abide here is *to take up residence; similar to a place to lodge permanently; to remain; stay*. To abide means to remain or stay with God and not leave Him at home when we go to work or other places.

11

People should be able to see Him in us at all times. Even when we are out with friends, it should be obvious He is in us. We don't participate in ungodliness.

Abiding is a big thing with God. In John 15:7, Jesus said that when we abide in Him and His words abide in us, we can ask what we will of Him, and it will be done. Psalm 91 contains some of His words that need to abide in us.

Under the shadow—This is a defensive place of protection. You can't get much closer than that to the Most High. We will be hard for the enemy to detect and impossible for the enemy to harm when we are close enough to be in God's shadow. We are instructed to draw near to God, and He will draw near to us (*see* James 4:8).

Of the Almighty (originates from two words: all and mighty)—God has all the might. There is none mightier! It is literally El Shaddai, another name of God that means *the Almighty*.

Genesis 17:1 is the first time El Shaddai is used when God is speaking to Abraham. In Genesis 17:2, Almighty God promised Abraham that if he would keep the conditions of the proceeding verse, He (God) will multiply him exceedingly—as the dust (*see* Gen. 13:16), as the stars (*see* Gen. 15:5), and as the sand (*see* Gen. 22:17).

According to the Dake Annotated Bible, the Almighty also means *Fruitful One*. God was to multiply Abraham abundantly. The Life-Giver was to restore life to Abraham and Sarah, whose bodies were as good as dead as far as offspring was concerned. Through Him, they were to have future offspring. This depicts God as the strong-nourisher, strength-giver, all-bountiful satisfier, and supplier of the needs of His people.

We've learned from this first verse of Psalm 91 that God expects us to choose to go to the secret place, and we are not to move from the nearness of Him. We are to take up residence in His presence and remain there. What better place is there to be? We are talking about the Most High and Almighty after all.

Psalm 91:2—*I will say of the Lord, He is my refuge and fortress: my God; in Him will I trust.*

Those who dwell here (under the shadow of the Almighty) should say something.

I (not the pastor, an evangelist, a parent, a friend, or anyone else)—This is your responsibility and only yours.

Many times in Scripture, God said, "If you do this, then I will do this." Just like we have to say and believe to be saved, we must be proactive in order to receive His protection. We are responsible for our own salvation, and we are responsible for our own protection. We do what we are supposed to do, and God does what He has promised. We cannot do His job, and He will not do ours for us.

Will say (you have something to do here)—Will you actually *say*, or will you just think, read, or mentally agree?

You may question, "Does He really expect me to say something?" Well, if we are to take Scripture literally, that IS what He has instructed. One of the rules of interpreting Scripture is to take it literally when we can. How simple it is to do just that? I think we are really missing it if we don't. I will continue to emphasize this point as we go.

In order to dwell in the secret place of the Most High and abide under the shadow of the Almighty, the Word of God states you will *say* something. It doesn't instruct that we can just read, mentally ascent, agree with, believe, or think this. It is unreasonable to think that God would mean we can just read it silently or just think about it when it clearly states to *say* (speak forth or declare) it.

Scripture indicates that Naaman (the leper) would have rather done some great thing than just go dip in the Jordan River seven times to be healed, as the prophet said for him to do (*see* 2 Kings 5:13). What *great thing* would you rather do than just say something? I've seen a lot of posts quoting one or more of the verses of Psalm 91 on social media. That doesn't guarantee protection or deliverance. Saying (declaring it with your mouth) is one of the requirements to activating this psalm in your life. Again, this is God's way, not mine. Matthew 12:37 helps to confirm my point: *For by thy words thou shall be justified, and by thy words thou shall be condemned.* I will let that verse speak for itself as to just how important our words are.

We need to keep control of our mouths. We must be careful not to speak contrary to the truth of the Word of God. *A man shall eat good by the fruit of his mouth: but the soul of transgressors shall eat violence. He that keeps his mouth keeps life: but he that opens wide his lips shall have destruction* (Prov. 13:2–3). I believe it means just what it says.

Read the above verses again and let them sink in. There are many other such verses that also give powerful instructions for the use of our mouth. We should take all of them seriously. The books of James and Proverbs are excellent places to get more understanding of how to use the mouth wisely.

Of the Lord (there is only one Lord)—Is He your Lord, or is He just a lord to you? It makes all the difference. Many people believe in the existence of a god, but do they believe in the one true God? And have they made Him their Lord? Again, it makes a difference. If He is not our Lord, He is not obligated to protect us.

What will you say of the Lord? This is important. You don't just say *anything* of Him. Do you say that God is your Lord, the Most High? Again, He is not the Almost High; He is the Most High. His name is not Some Might; His name is Almighty. He gives us the exact words to say. We cannot go wrong with proclaiming the truth of what He has instructed us to say.

He is my refuge (what one says of the Lord)—As believers, we say, "He is my Lord and my refuge or hiding place."

A refuge is a place of protection from all evil—men, pestilences, devils, sicknesses, diseases, hurricanes, tornados, or earthquakes. ALL evil. Is God your refuge? There is only one safe place in the world, and by speaking that God is your refuge, you are declaring that He is that safe place of protection for you.

It doesn't matter if you are in a fiery furnace or a lion's den; God is your protection. King Nebuchadnezzar threatened to throw Shadrach, Meshach, and Abednego into the burning fiery furnace because they would not fall down and worship the gold image that he had made (*see* Dan. 3). The three Jewish men neither cried out to God, begging Him to save them, nor did they complain and murmur against God. No, they trusted God and proclaimed, *Our God will deliver us!* I believe their words and faith saved them. For the three Hebrews, the furnace was just as safe as their bedroom. When the king saw that the fire had no power over them, he changed his decree to say that there was no other god than the Almighty.

King Darius issued an edict that no one could pray to any god or human besides himself. Because Daniel would not cease praying to the Most High, he was thrown into the lions' den (*see* Dan. 6). God protected him from being devoured by shutting the mouths of the furious beasts. When the king saw that the Almighty had protected Daniel, he issued a decree that all in his kingdom must fear and reverence the God of Daniel.

It doesn't matter if an army is pursuing you. In 2 Kings 6, we find Elisha surrounded by a host of horses and chariots. When Elisha's servant saw this, he became fearful, but Elisha told him not to fear. Elisha prayed for the Lord to open his servant's eyes, and he declared, *They that be with us are more than they that be with them.*

We can be faced with perilous circumstances, or we can be in dangerous places at any time. As we continue in Psalm 91, we'll see that God has all that covered too. All of the preparation you could think to do to ensure your safety couldn't possibly prevent everything that could happen, but God says He can. He is the ONLY one who can.

And my fortress—God is your (place of) protection. This fortress (God) IS your place of refuge.

When I was in the Navy, I was stationed in Puerto Rico for a while, and I had the opportunity to visit two forts in San Juan. The forts were not old wooden ones like you would see attacked and burned in an old Western on television. They were built of rock and mortar with walls six to eight feet thick. That's MY kind of impenetrable fortress! That's the kind of place a person can feel safe in, and God's place of refuge is so much more awesome than that.

Can you imagine God's fortress? It is impenetrable by any enemy.

My God—He is your God if Jesus is your Lord and Savior. Jesus may be *the* Savior, but have you made Him *your* Savior?

Since we are living under the New Testament covenant, we must go through Jesus (the only way) to get to God (*see* John 14:6). And we must be able to declare what Psalm 91:2 states. According to Romans 10:9 or a like scripture, He is our God only when we have accepted Jesus as our Lord and Savior. I was led to the Lord by Romans 10:9: *That if thou shalt confess with thy mouth* [this is saying something] *the Lord Jesus and believe* [this is faith] *in thine heart that God hath raised Him from the dead, thou shalt be saved.*

I recognize this verse as stating the same thing. It is confessing God as your Lord and trusting Him, which is faith. If you have confessed and believed by faith, according to Romans 10:9, you are saved. God accepts you as His son or daughter just as you are right now. Then you are able to proclaim in faith that you trust Him.

In Him will I trust (now you have said and agreed that you can trust Him)—This applies to all who will comply with it, and since He is our Father, we can trust Him.

If God asked us to do some great thing, like go to Jerusalem, in order to receive this kind of protection, how soon would we start saving up for the trip? He knows many people, sadly, would not make it. He expects us to simply believe what we say and what He says. That's where faith comes in—when we trust Him. When you say (decree) what this psalm states, you are, in effect, saying of the Lord that He is your refuge and fortress, and because He is your God, you can fully trust Him. Trust is a pivotal element that activates this psalm for you so you can expect God to do what He has promised.

Now that you are His, He obligates Himself to protect you in the following verses (3–16) of Psalm 91. Now we enter into His protection. How simple God made it just to believe and say, "He is my refuge and my fortress: my God; in Him will I trust."

An Audience with King Jesus

As I stated before, saying, believing (in faith), and trusting God is how you enter into, activate, and participate in Psalm 91. You can't just read, mentally ascent to, agree with, or even just think about it; He commanded that we must *say* it. We cannot leave this part out. He made it just that simple for us. It's the same way we are saved.

We are told to come boldly and ask God for anything. Whatever we ask, we will receive (*see* 1 John 3:22).

*Let us come boldly to the throne of grace,
that we may obtain mercy, and find grace
to help in time of need* (Heb. 4:16).

*Whatsoever you ask the Father in my name,
He will give it to you* (John 15:16; *see*
John 16:23).

Enter into the Holiest by the blood of Jesus
(Heb. 10:19).

*In whom we have boldness and access with
confidence by the faith of Him* (Eph. 3:12).

These scriptures reveal that we can have an audience with the Most High and Almighty at any time. What a privilege!

It would be very disrespectful and dishonorable not to take time to speak to the Most High and Almighty when He has specifically invited us. Even in the natural, there is a certain protocol for speaking to important people or dignitaries. If I had the opportunity to have an audience with someone of great importance, I wouldn't busy myself with mowing my lawn or indulge myself by eating popcorn while watching a ball game, would you? How rude! Especially if the opportunity was with someone in a position to do me a great favor, whatever I asked.

What if the president of the United States personally invited you to come boldly into his presence; to have full access to him; to have his full, undivided attention at any time? And what if he said that whatever you asked, he would do? (*see* Mark 11:23–24) I don't know about you, but I would surely respond to his offer.

Sadly, I don't think we fully grasp the significance of the incredible opportunity God affords us. Is God not declaring that he (anyone in Christ) who dwells in the secret place of the Most High and abides in the shadow of the Almighty has full access to Him?

What exactly would you *say* to the president of the United States if you had access to him? Would you pause to think about what you would actually say in his presence? I certainly wouldn't want to seem foolish or ignorant. I would definitely choose my words wisely.

The same is true with the Most High and Almighty, only all the more so.

Reflection

In your dwelling place, you don't just go and visit. As I noted previously, it's a place to lodge, have residence. People shouldn't be surprised to find you there. We dwell there by taking God's Word and claiming it, possessing it, and living it.

Why SAY? Because it's the factual and easiest way to receive something from God. He didn't ask us to accomplish some great feat in order to receive this protection. We would do it if He had, right?

This may seem just too easy, but it is the way God wants it, so we can't say we did something to earn it on our own. We also cannot say that it was too hard to achieve, and, therefore, we have no excuse for not doing as He commands.

The words representing God in the first two verses of Psalm 91 describe different aspects of His power to protect:

1. Most High (none higher) shows Him to be greater than any threat we face.

2. Almighty (all mighty) emphasizes His power to confront, defeat, and destroy every enemy. The enemies mentioned in this psalm don't have a chance against the Most High and Almighty!

3. The Lord, as the leader and authority in our lives, assures us that His presence and guidance are always with us. In these first two verses, we must proclaim Him to be our Lord in order for us to receive the protection of which He speaks.

4. God says that He is our God and that we have chosen Him. This expresses the truth that God has chosen to have a deep, personal relationship with those who trust (have faith) in Him.

The more we say these truths aloud, the more confident we become of His protection. Again, just mentally agreeing that the Lord is our refuge is not enough. Power is released in our words of faith when we say them aloud. By saying them in faith, we are placing our being in His shelter. By voicing our acceptance and reliance on His lordship and protection, we open the door to the secret place.

On a side note, I cannot emphasize enough to take careful note of what flies out of your mouth in times of trouble. Remember, our words have power! We have the ability to bless or to curse. Don't speak death and destruction—for example, "That just tickles me to death," or "You're killing me." SPEAK LIFE!

Cursing or even speaking forth things that you do not want or desire only makes matters worse. When I teach at the detention center, I always tell the attendees to never say what they don't want to happen. I encourage them to replace negative, destructive words with what they do want to happen. It can make a difference in the outcome. Give God something to work with. Speak life. Speak truth. Speak what you want and desire. *For he that will love life, and see good days, let him refrain his tongue from evil, and his lips that they speak no guile* (1 Peter 3:10).

God is four factors to us:

1. He is our refuge or hiding place.
2. He is our fortress or place of protection.
3. He is our true and faithful God.
4. We trust Him, and our security is in Him and Him alone.

Give us help from trouble: for vain is the help of man. God alone is our defense and protection (Ps. 60:11).

3

THE DEFENSIVE HAND OF GOD

THE REST OF Psalm 91 indicates God's part (His promises). God is actually offering us protection from anything and everything mentioned in Psalm 91. Let's take a look at from what He protects us.

> **Psalm 91:3—*Surely He shall deliver thee from the snare of the fowler and the noisome pestilence.***

We cannot be caught in a snare.

Surely (without a doubt; truly; most certainly) *He* (the Most High and Almighty) ***shall deliver thee*** (me; you) ***from the snare of the fowler*** (symbolic of any enemy that sets a trap)—Many times God delivers us from a snare even before we step into it, and we may not have even been aware of it.

This verse paints a picture of a person walking unsuspectingly into a snare that suddenly yanks him up off of his feet and slings him high into the air, leaving him hanging helpless and upside down. When God says He delivers us from the snare, we can expect such a delivery even before we step into it. How grateful we can be right now to know He obligates Himself to do that. Psalm 91:2 did state that we will trust Him.

The Lord is known by the judgement he executes: The wicked is snared by the work of his own hands (Ps. 9:16). I like this verse. The very snare that the enemy sets for you will trap him in return. However, this doesn't just happen automatically. This truth is only activated by making Jesus your Lord, by speaking or declaring the words (truth), and by having faith in those words. I will continue repeating this as we go along to make a solid point as to how to activate this psalm in your life.

And the noisome pestilence—The Dake Annotated Bible notes that this (noisome pestilence) is like a rushing calamity that sweeps everything before it. This brings to my mind a picture of a tsunami, tornado, or forest fire. God said He would deliver us from those as well.

How will He deliver us from these things? It could be as simple as not being in the wrong place at the wrong time. Being held up in traffic could prevent us from having an accident down the road. I don't complain about that anymore; I've seen what can happen.

> **Psalm 91:4—*He shall cover thee with His feathers, and under His wings shalt thou trust: His truth shall be thy shield and buckler.***

Trust God's truth as a shield.

He shall cover thee with His feathers, and under His wings shalt thou trust—This is figurative of the protection a mother hen gives her baby chicks. When a mother hen senses danger, she calls for her chicks by clucking, and they come running. This verse, in essence, protects us from evil, just as a mother hen protects her chicks from danger. When we sense danger, we should run to God. We do this by staying near Him and thanking Him for all the protection He provides in this psalm.

Compare this verse to when Jesus said of Jerusalem: *How often I would have gathered thy children together, as a hen doth gather her brood under her wings, and ye would not* (Luke 13:34). The Israelites did not allow Him to protect them. They had a choice, and so do we. We already made our choice in Psalm 91:1–2. We have executed these verses, and we trust God and His promises. Scripture warns us to not trust in servants, saints, friends, or riches, but we are told many times to trust only Him. No one is more trustworthy than God.

His truth shall be thy shield and buckler—According to Strong's Concordance, the definition of buckler is *something surrounding the person, like a shield that surrounds you like an impenetrable bubble.* Nothing can get through God's shield.

God's truth is always something we can count on. His Word is always true. It is like a shield that protects the vital parts of the body from arrows, spears, and any other kind of attack by the enemy.

We are to take up the shield of faith, with which we shall be able to quench all the fiery darts of the wicked one (*see* Eph. 6:16). Truth and faith are always shields, and they will be effective when used. Protection is activated by our words (God's truth) of faith.

4

WE SHALL NOT BE AFRAID

THERE ARE MANY things in this world that can cause alarm, but God commands us to fear NOT. Since this is a commandment, He expects us to deal with it the way He advises—do not fear. Remember, He never requires anything of us for which He will not provide the means! Since we are warned that fear will most certainly come knocking, trusting God now will help us deal with it when it does.

> **Psalm 91:5—***We shall not be afraid for the terror by night; nor for the arrow that flieth by day.*

The command to fear not.

We *shall not be afraid*—This is a command, but it is our choice whether or not we obey it. It always is.

In this verse and the next, God records four things to not fear. Again, YOU need to trust Him and not be afraid. Be secure and confident in the Most High and Almighty. Faith drives fear out. Fear and faith cannot lodge together. We choose one or the other. Faith is choosing not to fear.

But doesn't the Bible tell us to have fear? Yes, but we are only to have a reverent fear of God (*see* Matt. 10:28; Luke 12:5; 1 Peter 2:17; Rev. 14:7). Hebrews 4:1 indicates that only one type of fear IS good—fear of God's judgement. *Let us therefore fear, lest a promise being left us of entering into any rest, any of you should come short of it* (Heb. 4:1). A fear of not entering into eternal rest should cause us to be fearful enough of judgement. It should cause us to be faithful and obedient to God while being fearless of man and anything else in and of the world.

Fearing anything but God is not good. *For unto us was the Gospel preached, as well as unto them, but the Word preached did not profit them, not being mixed with faith* (Heb. 4:2). Those referred to in Hebrews 4:2 did not have enough fear of eternal judgement in order to be profitable, to produce faith mixed with the Word in them. Faith must be mixed with the Word of God to be profitable. As I mentioned, faith will not mix with fear.

We shall not be afraid for the terror by night—If we choose to not be afraid of the terror by night now and trust God, fear will have a harder time penetrating and taking up residence in our heart. Wicked people and devils use nighttime as a cloak to hide and do evil. We *say* we trust God to deliver us from the terror by night too.

Trusting God and walking in faith without fear has to be intentional, done on purpose. We cannot pretend evil does not prowl around like a roaring lion looking for someone to devour (*see* 1 Peter 5:8), yet we shall not be afraid.

We shall not be afraid...nor the arrow that flieth by day—
Arrows that fly by day is figurative of the dangers from the wicked (attacks) that happen during the daytime, when we are fully awake. Yes, these attacks are in broad daylight. These arrows, as applied to Christian warfare, can refer to various temptations, such as lusts of the flesh or ungodly thoughts that *fly by day* (when we are awake).

We should intentionally not fear these temptations. In fact, we are to use our shield of faith to quench them. *Above all taking the shield of faith, wherewith we shall be able to quench all the fiery darts of the wicked* (Eph. 6:16).

How do we do as this? When we realize we are being attacked, we can use (apply) the living Word of God, which is as sharp as a sword, like Jesus did when He was tempted. His answer to every temptation was: *It is written* (*see* Matt. 4:4–10; Luke 4:4–12)!

When Jesus was tempted, He applied the Word of God along with His shield of faith to avert the temptations (arrows). He actually spoke God's Word in faith to defeat the devil. That's how it's done. Even fiery arrows and spears were used as warfare in biblical times to damage and defeat the enemy. We can do the same thing with God's Word (Sword). That is why it is important to *know* what is written (the Word of God).

> **Psalm 91:6—***Nor for the pestilence that walketh in darkness; nor for the destruction that wasteth at noonday.*

Devastation happens all over the world, and we can never predict it, so where can we be safe from such devastation? In the shadow of the Almighty. *Who hath delivered us from the power of darkness...*(Col. 1:13).

*We shall not be afraid...nor the pestilence that walketh in darkness—*This pestilence seems to come during darkness. If you recall, pestilence is also mentioned in verse 3. God is trying to make a point.

According to Strong's Concordance, pestilence means *a plague*. A plague is a blow, an infliction, a spot (as on a leprous person), sore, striker, stroke, or wound. So, disease is definitely indicated here. Pestilence was used by God as a threat to destroy idol-worshipping

Israel, and it was actually used against Israel numerous times by God. The occurrence of pestilence is also one of the signs that we should look for before Jesus's second coming (*see* Matt. 24:7; Luke 21:11).

We shall not be afraid...nor for the destruction that wasteth at noonday—We choose. Strong's Concordance defines destruction as ruin, waste, and devastation. This brings to mind occurrences like earthquakes, fires, tornadoes, or floods that could happen quickly, without warning, and at any time.

Night or day, God said to fear not. There is good reason for this. Scripture supports the idea that fear will draw to us the things we do not want. *For the thing I greatly feared is come upon me, and that which I was afraid of is come unto me* (Job 3:25). Could fear be one reason why bad things happen to good people? Let that not be us.

Proverbs 29:25 adds support to this: *The fear of man brings a snare, but whoever puts his trust in the Lord will be safe.* So, fear can get us caught in the very snare from which God desires to deliver us. How ironic. Our fears can actually override His protection. It seems fear can be as powerful to stop the hand of God as faith is to move the hand of God. Think about that for a minute.

What makes the difference? We choose.

According to Proverbs 26:2, there is always a reason why bad things happen. *As the bird by wandering, as the swallow by flying, so the curse causeless shall not come.* It's not just bad luck, as some would say. Fear can invite or bring about devastation and ruin, and it can stop the hand of God's protection. The Bible makes it clear that the only thing to fear is God.

If you ever question whether or not whatever we may fear in this world is more powerful than God, be assured that greater is He who is in you than he who is in the world (*see* 1 John 4:4). Think about it.

5

God's Preservation and the Wicked's Defeat

THOUSANDS FALLING AROUND us could be something that provokes great fear, but God apprises us ahead of time just how to deal with it. Obedience always brings victory; therefore, by doing things His way, we will always be victorious. God's Word (when applied His way) always brings success.

> **Psalm 91:7**—*A thousand may fall at thy side, and ten thousand at thy right hand; but it shall not come nigh thee.*

You may be the last man standing. God is letting you know that there can be times when thousands could be falling all around you, but you are not to fear even then. *Yea, though I walk through the valley of the shadow of death, I will fear no evil...*(Ps. 23:4).

God preserves His beloveds. There are countless instances recorded in Scripture where God preserved His beloveds (when they were obedient and faithful to Him). Let's take a look at two particular cases:

> Noah: *Noah was a just man and perfect in his generations, and Noah walked with God* (Gen. 6:9). The word perfect here means *without blemish, without spot, or undefiled.* The same word is used forty-six times in the Bible when depicting the specified and required condition of sacrificial animals.
>
> During the great flood, Noah and his family were the only ones spared from the devastation (*see* Gen. 7:23). Thousands fell all around Noah and his family, but God saved them. There were

only eight people left of pure Adamic (perfect) stock.

Joshua and Caleb: *And now, behold the Lord has kept me alive, as He said, these forty and five years...*(Josh. 14:10). In this case, all the men of Israel forty years of age and older died in the wilderness during their forty years of wandering. Thousands, perhaps millions fell at their (Joshua and Caleb's) side, but as Psalm 91:7 states, death did not come near them.

Joshua and Caleb were the only two (out of twelve) who came back with a good report after spying out the land that God had commanded they take. It's no coincidence because only they spoke the word of God that was in their heart (*see* Num. 14:1–9). The other ten came back with a report of fear, asserting the giants were too numerous and mighty to defeat. Notice that Joshua and Caleb did not fear. And they were the only ones, who were forty years and older, who were able to enter into the promised land.

This is a testament of Caleb and Joshua's faith, obedience and long-suffering.

Caleb wholly followed the Lord (*see* Josh. 14:7–14). Caleb received the inheritance Moses said he could have, and God kept him just as strong as he was at the beginning of the wandering in the wilderness. There is no reason why God would not give Caleb that long to live to enjoy the inheritance he deserved. Joshua also lived a long life; he lived to be 110 years old.

Revelation 11:3 gives an example of a future promise not yet fulfilled of God preserving His chosen ones: *God will give power to His two witnesses, and they shall prophesy a thousand two hundred and three score days, clothed in sackcloth.* God declares these two witnesses will prophesy for three and a half years, and He will preserve them while their enemies die all around them.

The question is, can you believe this kind of divine protection for yourself? If you want to receive this kind of protection, you have no choice BUT to believe. Remember, these promises are only for those who know and believe His promises. *My people* [those who do not know His promises] *are destroyed for lack of knowledge: because thou* [those who do not believe His promises] *hast rejected knowledge, I will also reject thee* (Hos. 4:6). Therefore, just choose to believe and trust, and do not fear. That's faith! That is how we activate God's protection in Psalm 91.

Why does God choose to protect you while thousands fall around you? Because you have said He is your God (v. 2), you will trust Him (vv. 2, 4), and you will not fear (v. 5). As we learned, God is no respecter of persons, but He does respect your reverent fear of Him and your profession of faith.

> **Psalm 91:8—*Only with thine eyes shalt thou behold and see the reward of the wicked.***

What reward do I want? It's up to me.

Malachi 1:5 states: *And your eyes shall see, and ye shall say, "The Lord be magnified from the border of Israel."* And Genesis 6:5 states: *And God saw that the wickedness of man was great in the earth and that every imagination of the thoughts of his heart was only evil continually.* Note that it doesn't say that their words or actions were wicked. It only says that every imagination of the thoughts of their hearts was only evil continually.

Genesis 7:23 gives the account of the reward of the wicked in Noah's time: *Every living substance was destroyed which was upon the face of the ground...and Noah only remained alive, and they that were with him in the ark.* Only Noah and his family were left alive to see the reward of the wicked.

We have already noted that Joshua and Caleb saw the reward of the wicked. *And the whole congregation said unto them, "Would God that we had died in the land of Egypt! or would God we had died in this wilderness!"* (Num. 14:2) The Israelites who grumbled and murmured did die in the wilderness because they feared the giants and spoke against God. They were fearful and did not trust God—the two very things we are instructed to NOT do in Psalm 91. We are to speak truth and to fear not, just as Joshua and Caleb did (*see* Num. 14:31–33).

This is another example for the proper use of our words. It is glaringly obvious in hindsight that the Israelites should not have said what they did, especially to God. I'm sure that isn't what they really wanted, but it IS what they said. They had what they spoke.

Have you ever said something you didn't really mean or want to happen? Guard your words because you might just get what you say.

The point here is that those in the days of Noah and the Israelites in the wilderness were wicked in the thoughts of their hearts, yet Noah and his family and Joshua and Caleb witnessed their reward because of it.

God searches the hearts of men. *Search me, O God, and know my heart; try me, and know my thoughts: And see if there be any wicked way in me, and lead me in the way everlasting* (Ps. 139:23–24). It is important to note here that while it is most valuable and good to examine your own heart and repent from any wickedness God exposes, do not let condemnation creep in. In God's great mercy and grace, we are to receive conviction and instruction, which leads us to repentance (*see* Rom. 2:4).

Be reminded that there is no condemnation to those who are in Christ Jesus (*see* Rom. 8:1).

6

GOD'S PROTECTION AND POWER

WHEN WE HAVE fulfilled the requirements of God (our part), we can expect Him to do His part without fail. God will be faithful to move mightily on our behalf. Knowing, believing, and living out this promise gives us divine peace, freedom, and protection that the world simply cannot offer.

> **Psalm 91:9–10—***Because thou hast made the Lord, which is my refuge, even the Most High, thy habitation; there shall no evil befall thee, neither shall any plague come nigh thy dwelling.*

No plague, no plague, no plague!

I decided to link these two verses (vv. 9–10) together because the first verse is incomplete without the second. Verse 10 is an incomprehensible promise that needs to go with the preceding verse.

Because thou hast made the Lord, which is my refuge, even the Most High, thy habitation—Because you have done what is required (you have made God your Lord, and you dwell with Him) in the first two verses of Psalm 91, God will do something. If you had not done what was your responsibility, God could not fulfill His promise to you in verse 10.

There shall no evil befall thee—I see this as all-encompassing. If God hadn't said anything before now, this right here would be good enough. What else does He need to say? He promises even more.

Neither shall any plague come nigh your dwelling—Wow! Talk about a timely promise! The plagues described previously in verses 3 and 6 can't even come near our dwellings!

This protection seems to be more encompassing than just our own individual being. This appears to be offering protection for those within our dwelling as well—our family! Well, it's not the first time God offered to protect a family of the righteous. We just learned in the account of Noah how God saved his whole family, but are there others? Is there a pattern here?

In Joshua 2:12, Rahab made the two spies promise to show kindness to her father's house. Then she requested that they would save her whole household. *And that ye will save alive my father, and my mother, and my brethren, and my sisters, and all they have, and deliver our lives from death* (Josh. 2:13). In Joshua 6:23, we see that they and all theirs were saved because Rahab asked for them to be protected, and they were.

Two angels came to destroy Sodom and to save Lot. According to 2 Peter 2:7, Lot was a righteous man. After some time in Lot's house, the angels told Lot to leave and take his wife and daughters with him so they wouldn't be destroyed with the city (*see* Gen. 19:12). They were warned and protected.

Joshua said that he and his house would serve the Lord (*see* Josh. 24:15). Therefore, I surmise that Joshua's whole house could receive God's protection through him.

In Acts 16:30–31, Paul's jailer was told words by which he and his household could be saved. Even though they would have to make their own individual choices to receive Jesus as their Lord and Savior, it seems they could be protected.

Based on these instances, it appears that God wants us to know that His protection will extend into our whole household. Our loved ones can and will receive the same protection.

There are many testimonies of this psalm being prayed over sons and husbands who went off to war and came back without a scratch. I have a personal testimony of a son who was in the Marines. He completed tours in Iraq and Afghanistan. We professed Psalm 91 over him and his platoon, and they all came back without a scratch. God keeps His promises for our households, for those in our dwelling.

Psalm 91:11—*For He shall give His angels charge over thee, to keep thee in all thy ways.*

Angels are waiting for your words.

As if God hasn't said enough to make it perfectly clear that He wants to protect us from the snare of the fowler, noisome pestilence, night terrors, arrow that flies by day, pestilence in darkness and destruction at noonday, thousands falling all around us, all evil (that cannot touch us), and any plague (that cannot come near our place of dwelling), now God has given His angels charge over us, to protect and keep us in all our ways.

The angel of the Lord encamps round about them that fear Him, and delivers them (Ps. 34:7). Some people don't fear God, and, as we've learned, this can lead to their own destruction. The fear of God seems to qualify "them" for deliverance here. Angels can and will protect us from anything and everything under certain conditions. Fearing God is one of those conditions.

Hebrews 1:14 says of angels: *Are they not all ministering spirits sent forth to minister for them who shall be heirs of all salvation*? We are heirs because of verses 1 and 2, right?

Prayer can get angels involved. *Peter therefore was kept in prison: but prayer was made without ceasing of the church unto God for* [Peter] *him* (Acts 12:5). One example of deliverance is when an angel of the Lord delivered Peter from chains and helped him escape from prison (*see* Acts 12:7–11). An angel woke Peter up and told him to follow him. The angel then led him to the street and left. After the occurrence, Peter finally realized the angel had been sent to deliver him.

Are we giving our assigned angels something to do when we speak God's Word, or are we, in effect, tying their hands when we speak contrary to His Word? Are they waiting for our voice to speak His Word? Think about it.

In Hebrews 12:33, Paul reminded us how through faith, Daniel obtained God's promises: *My God hath sent his angel, and hath shut the lions' mouths, that they have not hurt me...*(Dan. 6:22). And 2 Kings 6:16-17 gives an account of the mountain full of horses and chariots of fire round about Elijah. Angels are always there; we just can't always see them.

> **Psalm 91:12—***They shall bear thee up in their hands, lest thou dash thy foot against a stone.*

What do angels do?

Though he falls, he shall not utterly be cast down: for the lord upholders him with his hand (Ps. 37:24). Here, even God gets involved to save the righteous. He doesn't even want us to bruise our foot on a stone. How thoughtful. Hasn't He thought of everything? But wait, there's more!

7

POWER OF ATTORNEY

I LIKE THE THOUGHT of putting my foot on the devil's head and trampling him under my feet. Christ has already given those who are His own the power and authority to defeat the enemy. There is nothing the devil or any principality of darkness can do about it, and, therefore, we have nothing to fear.

> **Psalm 91:13—***Thou shall tread upon the lion and adder: the young lion and the dragon thou shall trample under feet.*

The safe place for Daniel was in the lion's den!

In order to tread and trample on the enemy, we cannot walk in fear. These are things that strike fear in most of us. Peter charged us: *Be sober, be vigilant; because your adversary the devil, as a roaring lion, walks about seeking whom he may devour* (1 Peter 5:8). Our enemy cannot devour just anyone. He is looking for the weak and fearful ones. He's looking for the ones who wander away from the flock. The Shepherd cannot protect those who wander away from the flock.

Daniel 6 details the account of Daniel's victory in the lion's den. King Darius established a decree that no one ask a petition of any god for thirty days. Daniel knew when the writing was signed, but he went into his house, opened the windows toward Jerusalem, and kneeled down and gave thanks three times a day, just as he had done before. Verse 16 tells us that King Darius had Daniel cast into the den of lions, but verse 22 tells us that God sent an angel to shut the lions' mouths. When the king saw that Daniel hadn't been hurt, he changed his decree. *I make a decree that in every dominion of my kingdom men must tremble and fear before the God of Daniel…*(Dan. 6:26). The safe place for Daniel was in the lion's den.

So, let's talk about the power and authority over Satan and satanic powers that Jesus gives us under the New Testament covenant. If they had these in the Old Testament, surely we have them in the New Testament.

> *And Jesus came and spoke to them, saying, "All power is given unto me in heaven and earth. Go ye therefore, and teach all nations, baptizing them in the name of the Father, and of the Son, and of the Holy Ghost: Teaching them to observe all things whatsoever I have commanded you: and, lo, I am with you always, even to the end of the world." Amen* (Matt. 28:18–20).

Jesus gives us the power to do all that He commanded. He said He would always be with us. We cannot be fearful or doubtful and walk in the power and authority He has given us.

What power and authority have we been given? We have the power of attorney to use God's name. It's the same as Jesus doing it. *In my name shall they cast out devils...*(Mark 16:17). This is the ultimate power of attorney, the power to use God's name to do what He would do in our place. This also means that we have power and authority over devils that are using people to do their work. We have the authority to bind the devils and cast them out.

In John 14:14, Jesus said that if we ask anything in His name, He will do it. Again, this is Jesus expressing His willingness to allow us to use His name. Jesus said if we abide in Him and His words abide in us, we can ask for whatever we will, and it will be done for us (*see* John 15:7). This verse has a unique qualifier in that we must abide in Him, but we are already doing that, right? This verse sounds a lot like Psalm 91:13. We have been given power to tread on all the power of the enemy. Lions, snakes, and dragons are the enemy we should be treading on.

8

God's Deliverance and Provision

It is God's desire for us to have a long and healthy life. He tells us just how, and He assures us that if we do our part, He will do His. Because He loves us, God is available to bring us help at any time, day or night, wherever we may be.

> **Psalm 91:14—***Because he hath set his love upon Me, therefore will I deliver him: I will set him on high, because he hath known My name.*

Do you know His name?

I like the first word *because*. Because we have done something, God will do something. As you can see by now, that is how Psalm 91 works. This is another conditional blessing. When we do what is required, He provides the protection. When the Almighty says it, that's the best guarantee we can get in this world!

He hath set his love on me, therefore I will deliver him—John 14:15 is evidence of our love for Him: if we love Him, we will keep His commandments. Also notice the tense of this verse. We have already begun something, as noted in the use of present perfect tense. You (we) *hath (have)* set your (our) love upon Him. This tense designates an action that began in the past, but the effect of the action continues into the present. God also promises to deliver us in the future, and that's what faith is. I believe He will deliver on His promise.

I like Psalm 18:48: *He delivers me from my enemies: yea thou lift me up above those that rise up against me: thou hast delivered me from the violent man.* This is another scripture supporting this verse. David got delivered.

Love is a commandment. This is the great commandment of which Jesus spoke in Matthew 22:37: *Thou shall love the Lord thy God with all thy heart, and with all thy soul, and with all thy mind.* Why shouldn't we or why wouldn't we love God? He loves us unconditionally (*see* John 3:16).

Who else can deliver us? It is God's desire to deliver each one of us, but it is all up to us in what we say and do to get delivered. As I said, if we do something, God does what He said He would do. He cannot lie.

Let's take a moment to review what God has delivered and protected us from and what He has provided for us by what we have said and done:

1. The terror by night
2. Arrow that flies by day
3. Pestilence that walks in darkness
4. Destruction that wastes at noonday
5. No evil shall befall us
6. Neither shall any plague come near our dwelling
7. Angels keep us in all of our ways
8. We won't dash our foot against a stone

9. We trample on the lion, adder, and that
   old dragon

These are all forms of protection and provision by the Most High and Almighty. Who else could do this? Is there really anything else He needs to protect us from?

I will set him on high—Psalm 18:48 says that God lifts us up above the violent man. I also like Ephesians 2:6, which supports all this: *And has raised us up together, and made us sit together in heavenly places in Christ Jesus.*

So, when God says He will set us on high, this is an awesome place of power and authority. We can't get any higher than that, and we don't need to be. When you read, *I will set him on high*, just imagine sitting with Jesus in power and authority because that is where you are. Just how awesome is that?

Because he hath known My name—Again, because we have done something, God does something. It doesn't mean just because we know His name. Many people know God's name, yet they do not personally know Him as His names, and they haven't made Jesus their Lord and Savior; therefore, they do not have His protection.

> **Psalm 91:15**—*He shall call upon me, and I will answer him: I will be with him in trouble; I will deliver him, and honour him.*

God always answers. Count on it.

If this was the only verse in Psalm 91, it would be good enough. I know I've said that before about other verses, but it's true!

He shall call upon me—God never sleeps or slumbers, so we can call upon Him day or night. *He that keepeth thee will not slumber* (Ps. 121:3).

And I will answer—This is not like calling your kid who may or may not answer. God will always answer!

And all things whatsoever you ask in prayer, believing you shall receive (Matt. 21:22). In Mark 9:23, Jesus said that if we can believe, all things are possible.

And whatsoever ye shall ask in My name, that will I do, that the Father may be glorified in the Son (John 14:13).

There are numerous other scriptures regarding God's promise to answer us. There are also many scriptures that affirm He has already answered us.

I will be with him in trouble—Your best friend may not come to your aid when you are in trouble, but the Most High and Almighty can and will, always. God is in the business of rescuing His beloveds, even when we have had a hand in our own predicament.

King David said of the Lord: *For He has delivered me out of all trouble: and my eye has seen His desire upon my enemies* (Ps. 54:7). This is an example of God already having delivered someone, and David's eye had seen it (reference to Psalm 91:8). Sound familiar?

Psalm 59:16 is another allusion to verses 2 and 9 of Psalm 91, where we claimed God is our refuge: *For thou hath been my defense and refuge in the day of my trouble.*

The lord also will be a refuge for the oppressed, a refuge in times of trouble (Ps. 9:9).

I give you these verses so you can know that the Word of God is always in agreement with itself, and it helps to better understand when it is given in more than one example.

And I will honour him—And why would God honor us after all this? Because that's what He chooses to do. Jesus said that if any man serves Him, His Father will honor him (*see* John 12:26). *For them that honour Me I will honour...*(1 Sam. 2:30). Imagine God Almighty honoring us. And He tells us why He will—if we serve and honor Him.

> **Psalm 91:16**—*With long life will I satisfy him, and shew him My salvation.*

Because we have been protected from all the things our Father promised, we make it to a long life, and we are satisfied.

With long life will I satisfy him—Because of the previous verses that we do and He does, we get long life.

He asked life of thee, and thou gave it to him, even length of days for ever and ever (Ps. 21:4).

In 1 Kings 3:14, God told King Solomon: *If thou will walk in my ways, to keep my statutes and my commandments, as thy father David did walk, then I will lengthen thy days.* See, long life for us is God's will, and we have a lot to do with how long we live. Simply put, it all depends on what we say and do.

And shew him my salvation—Shew does not just mean *show* here. It means to experience, to present, and to provide us with His salvation. Strong's Concordance states that the word salvation here means *save; deliverance; aid; health; help; welfare.* God will present or provide His deliverance, aid, and anything else we need.

Reflection

Do you see now that there are certain conditions attached to God's blessings? And how people are destroyed for lack of or rejecting knowledge? Some lack knowledge because they have rejected it.

It seems God is going to great lengths to tell us of His protection that He has made available to us. Scripture says He made it available, but it is conditional on what we do and say. Although God desires everyone to be protected, it can only be received according to Scripture.

Can we avoid calamities, accidents, sicknesses, plagues, pestilences, and evil men used of the devil or even the devil himself? Not on our own.

We know there is no safe place in the world except in the secret place of the Most High, abiding under the shadow of the Almighty. In Him, I will trust. There is security in trusting God (Jehovah Rohi) completely. He will be our protection anywhere and at any time, day or night, when we activate it.

9

Conditions and Promises

I SAID IN THE beginning that I would give you a complete list of the conditions of God's promises as well as God's twenty-three promises found in Psalm 91.

Conditions of God's Promises

1. When you dwell in the secret place of the Most High, you abide under the shadow of the Almighty (v. 1).
2. Say and affirm that God is your refuge (v. 2).
3. Say and affirm that God is your fortress (v. 2).

4. Say and affirm that God is your God (v. 2).

5. Say and affirm that you trust God (vv. 2, 4).

6. Have faith and confidence that God will deliver you from every snare, trap, and pestilence (v. 3).

7. Have confidence in His protection (v. 4).

8. Trust His truth as your shield and buckler (v. 4).

9. Do not fear! Do not fear any night of terror, arrow by day, destruction, or pestilence. These listed here are literally things that the evil ones do to try to strike fear into you and destroy you (vv. 5–6).

10. Have faith and confidence in God that the plagues of people dying all around you will not come near your dwelling, though you will see it (vv. 7–8).

11. Reaffirm that God is your refuge (v. 9).

12. Make and reaffirm that God is your habitation (v. 9).

13. Set your love on Him (v. 14).

14. You know His name—Jehovah Rohi—your protector as the Good Shepherd (v. 14).

15. Call upon Him in prayer (v. 15).

These are very simple to apply. You will feel your faith rising as you say and do them.

23 Promises of God

1. You shall abide under the shadow of the Almighty (v. 1).
2. Surely God will deliver you from the snare of the fowler (v. 3).
3. Surely God will deliver you from the noisome pestilence (v. 3).
4. God will cover you with His feathers (v. 4).
5. His truth shall be your shield and buckler (v. 4).
6. You will not be afraid of the terror by night (v. 5).
7. You will not be afraid of the arrow that flies by day (v. 5).
8. You will not be afraid of the pestilence that walks in darkness (v. 6).
9. You will not be afraid of destruction at noon (v. 6).
10. Though a thousand fall at your side or ten thousand at your right hand, it shall not come near you (v. 7).

11. Only with your eyes you will see the reward of the wicked (v. 8).

12. There shall no evil befall you (v. 10).

13. There shall no plague come near your dwelling. This protection is for your family too (v. 10).

14. God will give His angels charge over you, to keep you in all your ways (v. 11).

15. Angels will bear you up their hands, lest you dash your foot against a stone (v. 12).

16. You will tread on the lion, the adder, the young lion, and the dragon (v. 13).

17. God will deliver you (vv. 14–15).

18. God will set you on high (v. 14).

19. God will answer you (v. 15).

20. God will be with you in trouble (v. 15).

21. God will honor you (v. 15).

22. God will satisfy you with long life (v. 16).

23. God will show you His salvation (v. 16).

Psalm 91 won't work and you won't know if it works unless you work it. If you work it, I believe you will live a very long and satisfied life.

Here is the way I look at it—if it doesn't work for us, it's because we missed it, not because of God. Too often, people want to point their finger at God and say, "I tried that, and it didn't work."

Again, I refer to the Word of God. *For what if some did not believe? Shall their unbelief make the faith of God without effect? God forbid: yea, let God be true, but every man a liar; as it is written, That thou might be justified in thy sayings, and might overcome when thou art judged* (Rom. 3:3–4). I think this speaks for itself.

As I said in the beginning, I don't want to complicate it. My goal is to unveil it by giving you the whole picture and by showing you how to receive the promises provided in Psalm 91. I'm just laying out how it is done and how you can do it.

Jesus told us that even a small amount of faith is powerful. *If you have faith as a grain of mustard seed, you shall say to this mountain, "Remove hence to yonder place;" and it shall remove; and nothing shall be impossible unto you* (Matt.17:20).

It seems we sometimes think just the opposite. Faith the size of a mountain can move a mustard seed.

We vastly underestimate the power of faith. When we understand that mustard seed faith is more like a nuclear bomb, we begin to get the picture. Now, that will move a mountain!

Jesus reprimanded His disciples when they lacked faith. One example is when a great storm of wind and waves beat upon their boat until it was full of water. Jesus was asleep on a pillow in the hinder part of the boat. When His disciples woke Him up and informed Him that they were about to perish, He rebuked the wind, and said to the sea, *Peace, be still.*

The wind ceased, and there was a great calm. Jesus then said to them, *Why are you so fearful? How is it you have no faith?* (*see* Mark 4:37–40)

Here is a classic case in point of faith being nonexistent when fear is present. The disciples were afraid they would perish; *they feared exceedingly.* Jesus indicated that they should have had faith and that they should have used it themselves. Jesus did say that the works that He did, we shall do also (*see* John 14:12).

According to Romans 12:3, we all have been given a measure of faith: *God has dealt to every man the measure of faith*. Surely, we all have *mustard seed* faith. Let's use what we have. The only faith we have to use is to believe God. We have to trust Him with our eternal life. We can use that same faith now and trust Him for our protection in this life.

God hasn't left anything out. God's Word is true and simply must be acted on according to the conditions of this psalm in order to be activated in our lives.

I hope you read this book with an open mind, and I hope you will apply it to your life. I believe you will be very happy with the results. Do the conditions, receive the promises, and expect God to do what He said. That's *mustard seed* faith. Use it. The blessings of the Lord are contingent on whether we act upon them or not. It's all up to you, not God. Do your part, and God will be faithful to do His.

10

CHOOSE LIFE

IF YOU HAVEN'T made Jesus your Lord and Savior yet, now is the time. God wants you to choose Him as your Lord and Savior and as your protector, as written in this psalm. He has already chosen you; now it's your turn.

God warned Israel through Moses: *I call heaven and earth to record this day against you, that I have set before you life and death, blessing and cursing: therefore choose life, that both thou and thy seed may live* (Deut. 30:19). God gave them the answer: choose life. God warned them again through Joshua: *Choose you this day whom you will serve...but, as for me and my house, we will serve the Lord* (Josh. 25:15).

I was on the way to a pastor's house August 29, 1986. I had decided that I wanted to get saved. I knew that believing was important and necessary; so, on the way there, I just decided to believe in Him. When I arrived at the pastor's house, I was invited in. When I told him that I wanted to talk about being saved, he opened his Bible to Romans 10:9 and said, "Read that."

I read out loud. *That if thou shalt confess with thy mouth the Lord Jesus, and shalt believe in thine heart that God hath raised him from the dead, thou shalt be saved.*

He then asked me if I believed what I had just read. I said that I did. Then he asked me if I was saved. When I said that I wasn't sure, he told me to read it again. I did. He asked, "According to what you just read and said, are you saved?"

I had to say yes at the time, but I still wasn't sure. It just seemed too easy. But that is the way it's done. It is still working today, thirty-three years later.

What I have done since is renew my mind to the Word of God, according to Romans 12:2: *And be not conformed to this world: but be ye transformed by the renewing of your mind, that you may prove what is that good, and acceptable, and perfect will of God.*

Just keep reading, studying, and doing the Word of God. It seems many Christians don't do these things after they are saved. Salvation is just the beginning of an exciting life for the "doer" of the Word of God.

If you haven't done this yet, just do it. It never fails to work. Contact me and tell me of your experience. Peter said to Jesus, *Lord, to whom shall we go? Thou hast the words of eternal life* (John 6:68).

I am the Lord, and there is none else, there is no god besides Me...(Isa. 45:5).

11

FINAL THOUGHTS

Reading Psalm 91 in the first person, as I've written it below, will help keep your battery charged, and it will prevent you from running out of gas. You can actually feel the promises and provisions working. The more you read it, the more faith will come. You will actually feel Romans 10:17 at work: *Faith comes by hearing and hearing by the Word of God.* I would say this daily until it becomes a part of your spirit!

Psalm 91 Personalized

I dwell in the secret place of the Most High and under the shadow of the Almighty.

I say of the Lord, You are my refuge and my fortress, my God. In You I will trust.

Surely You will deliver me from the snare of the fowler and the noisome pestilence.

You shall cover me with Your feathers, and under Your wings I will trust. Your truth shall be my shield and buckler.

I will not be afraid of the terror by night. I will not be afraid of the arrow that flies by day.

I will not be afraid of pestilence that walks in darkness. I will not be afraid of destruction that wastes at noonday.

A thousand may fall at my side, ten thou-sand at my right hand; but it will not come near me.

Only with my eyes shall I behold and see the reward of the wicked.

Because I have made You, Lord, my refuge and my habitation, no evil shall befall me, and no plague shall come near my dwelling.

For You, Lord, shall give Your angels charge over me, to keep me in all my ways.

They shall bear me up in their hands, so I won't dash my foot against a stone.

I will tread on the lion and the adder. The young lion and the dragon shall I trample under my feet.

Because I have set my love on You, You will deliver me. You will set me on high because I have known Your name.

I will call upon You, and You will answer me. You will be with me in trouble. You will deliver me, and honor me.

With long life You will satisfy me, and You will show me Your salvation.

Thanks be to God who has made this provision possible.

AUTHOR BIOGRAPHY

HERMAN (DUSTY) SHELTON is an ordained minister, a student of Dominion Bible Institute, and a certified divine healing technician of John G. Lakes Ministries, Curry Blake, as general overseer. Dusty has ministered at his local detention center for over twenty years, releasing God's love and presence while leading men to the Lord and making disciples of them. He has abandoned himself to the Holy Spirit and freely uses his God-given gifts and deep spiritual insights to help and encourage others to mature in Christ. Dusty is a dedicated husband, father, and grandfather, and he and his wife Carolyn live in central Arkansas.

Synopsis: Activating God's Protection

HAVE YOU EVER wondered if there is any place in the world that is safe from all the mounting dangers in this increasingly chaotic world? There is a safe place that you and your household can find refuge, where you can reside, and where you can find peace and rest. God reveals just where that security can be found in Psalm 91.

This book is not just about how to survive plagues and sicknesses or about how to survive catastrophes and threats like fires, floods, riots, or wars. There are specific conditions that must be met in order for the promises of God to manifest in our lives. In His infinite wisdom, God has provided all the instruction we need in just sixteen verses. This revelatory, step-by-step guide offers applicable spiritual understanding of how to access, unlock, and activate God's twenty-three promises and blessings of protection found in Psalm 91.

The Bible instructs us that we are not to fear anything in or of this world. Learning how to activate all of God's promises in Psalm 91 will empower you to break free from the fears of this world and receive by faith God's protection anywhere and at any time.

CPSIA information can be obtained
at www.ICGtesting.com
Printed in the USA
BVHW081923100921
616545BV00001B/159

9 781662 825620